Wherever You Are
You're Always Near Your Car

A Disaster Preparedness Guide

DJ Castle

Cover photos courtesy of the following:

Earthquake: "Kaiser Permanente Building After Northridge Earthquake" by Gary B. Edstrom - Photo by Gary B. Edstrom. Transferred from earlier upload at en.wikipedia. Licensed under Public domain via Wikimedia Commons – *http://commons.wikimedia.org/wiki/File:Kaiser_Permanente_Building_After _Northridge_Earthquake.jpg#mediaviewer/File:Kaiser_Permanente_Building _After_Northridge_Earthquake.jpg*

Evacuation: "I-45 & Louetta Rita Evacuation" by Ashish from Houston, TX - I-45 & louetta... Rita Evacuation. Licensed under Creative Commons Attribution 2.0 via Wikimedia Commons - *http://commons.wikimedia.org/ wiki/File:I-45_%26_Louetta_Rita_Evacuation.jpg#mediaviewer/File:I-45_%26 _Louetta_Rita_Evacuation.jpg*

Fire: Reuters/Mike Stone

Hurricane: National Oceanic and Atmospheric Administration/ Department of Commerce

Mudslide: National Oceanic and Atmospheric Administration/ Department of Commerce, The National Weather Service Albuquerque, NM, Pete Sanchez, Gary B. Edstrom

ISBN-13: 978-1502557452
ISBN-10: 1502557452

CONTENTS

DEDICATION

To Preppers Everywhere

- They read, write, surf the net, meet, talk and sometimes argue about the best ways to survive any disaster.

- They reach out, helping others to understand why they must prepare and then help them do so.

- They know that if you can take care of yourself, no one else has to take care of you.

- They'll take care of themselves, no matter what.

- They'll find a way to survive, no matter what.

Thank you.

Introduction

EMERGENCY PREPAREDNESS comes natural to me. Even as a child, I stored extra candy in my nightstand – just in case.

Decades later, grown and on my own, hearing predictions of food shortages and economic collapse, I felt the need to stock up – just in case.

I accumulated thirty-three 5-gallon cans of beans, rice, dry milk, wheat...and never used any of it. Nothing ever happened and I got tired of hauling it around with me whenever I moved, so I gave it to neighbors and friends and decided to change my ways.

It didn't last. Whether canned food or bottles of water, I always felt I should have "extras" on hand – just in case.

On May 18, 1980, Mount St. Helens erupted. Rivers flooded; people died, and while I wasn't near enough to fully experience the effect, it was a wakeup call. I began attending Red Cross seminars, studying everything I could find about disaster planning. I even started my own disaster kit company. It didn't get off the ground, but *I* was ready for anything.

In the 90's I rented a small house that had absolutely no storage space. One day while trying to locate something in a bedroom closet, my rolled up sleeping bag fell off the top shelf. No matter how I put it back, it wanted to roll around and end up on the floor. It was maddening, really. I began considering other places in the house where it could be stored, but came up empty.

Just as I was about to rope it in place, I realized it shouldn't be in the bedroom in the first place, where bed, blankets and comforter were more than adequate. Its purpose was for snuggling against outdoor elements; its best place for that sleeping bag was in my car.

Emergency preparedness pamphlets suggest having a blanket in the car, which may be fine if you live in southern California, but where I live, you'd need a lot more warmth than one blanket could provide.

If I were stranded in my car, I'd want that sleeping bag to be there with me – not at home.

As I began thinking it through, I realized there were other items I'd rather have in my car than at the house: camping gear, tools, rope, even my tent. It just made more sense to store them in the trunk – that's where they'd be needed if I were in my car when an emergency occurred.

A lot of preparedness information focuses on our homes, and it really does make sense to have survival items in one place where you can find them easily. You don't want to have to search for a flashlight in the dark after a 7.0 earthquake!

But how often are we at our homes?

Think about it: you get up in the morning and get ready for work, your car's in the garage. You get to work and it sits outside waiting for you. On the way home, you stop for groceries, gas, pizza – it's there with you. And while you sleep, your car is right outside, waiting for the cycle to begin again.

We're more often near our car than any other place! Odds are, for most of us, when an emergency happens, we'll be in or near our cars.

That's the focus of this guide. If we're at home when a disaster hits, we've got the luxury of our pantries, bedding, tools – you name it. But what if we're not at home? What should we be carrying in our cars so we can survive a disaster long enough to get back to those luxuries?

How to use this Guide

This is not a book about lists. It will engage your thinking, providing you with scenarios that could be very real – all from the viewpoint of dealing with them *from your car.*

Read a chapter, and then put yourself into each disaster scene. Think through what *you* would do and what *you* would want to have.

As you do, you'll see that if you're going to be prepared, you should prepare your car first.

Wherever you are, you're always near your car.

Good Luck and Good Reading!

Best,
DJ Castle

CHAPTER 1

Earthquakes and Fires and Floods. Oh My!

THERE'S BEEN AN EARTHQUAKE and you need to get home," lectured an emergency preparedness speaker. "If you need to drive from here to Lynnwood, 14 miles away, without crossing a single bridge, what roads would you take?"

The Community Emergency Response Team[1] seminar in Washington State began with that challenge question. We were surprised to learn that only one such route was possible.

Everett, Washington has a land area of 32.5 square miles, a population of 103,000 and *117 bridges!* I travel to or through it several times a week. When those bridges are damaged by a disaster such as an earthquake, how am I going to get home?

Why is this important to you? From a whopping 48,492 bridges in Texas to the mere 247 in the District of Columbia, your state has bridges.[2] Might there be one between *your* home and *your* work?

Many of these bridges are so much a part of the highway we don't even know we're crossing one, but they're there and after a major earthquake could be damaged beyond use.

How are you going to get home?

Power Lines: there are more than 500,000 miles of high–voltage transmission lines in the U.S. with hundreds of thousands more miles of distribution lines carrying electricity to our homes.[3] In a disaster, many of these lines will fall and if they're in your path, you aren't going anywhere.

Earthquakes, mudslides, fire and floods: these all have the same potential – they can alter the ground so extremely you will literally be stopped: can't go forward, can't go back.

In a rural area, trees could topple, creating a box from which the only way out is on foot. In an urban setting, bricks, glass and concrete from surrounding buildings will likewise block your route.

If you're away from home when an emergency occurs, you'll be dependent upon the contents of your car. You won't be able to rely on markets for food and supplies; you'll have only what you've put in your car ahead of time.

If you're at home when it happens, you may be forced to evacuate the area immediately – in your car.

In either case, your car becomes a valuable asset – if you've prepared it to be one.

From having enough gas in the tank to the supplies in the trunk, your car can be an oasis in the desert.

If you're going to prepare, prepare your car first!

References:

[1] http://www.ready.gov/community-emergency-response-teams-cert

"The Community Emergency Response Team (CERT) program helps train people to be better prepared to respond to emergency situations in their communities. When emergencies happen, CERT members can give critical support to first responders, provide immediate assistance to victims, and organize spontaneous volunteers at a disaster site.

"CERT training includes disaster preparedness, disaster fire suppression, basic disaster medical operations and light search and rescue operations."

For more information or to locate a CERT program:
http://www.fema.gov/community-emergency-response-teams

[2] http://www.statemaster.com/graph/trn_bri_tot_num-transportation-bridges-total-number

[3] http://www.ngridenergyworld.com/esw/html/teachers2.html#q5

Notes

CHAPTER 2

Test Yourself

HERE'S A DISASTER SITUATION for you to consider. Next chapter I'll offer some suggestions, but for now, I invite you to think it through with what you now know.

Imagine: what would you do? How would you do it? What would you need?

The more you put yourself into the scene, the more you'll gain from it. Try and be there for a few moments. Experience the situation and imagine how you would feel. Alarmed or terrified? Energized or frantic?

You're driving home after visiting a friend who lives only about thirty minutes away, but really in the boonies. You had a great time, staying a bit longer than planned, and as a result, it's 5:00 pm and getting dark.

It isn't raining or snowing but it's cloudy. The autumn evening is getting chilly and your car's heater is blowing welcome warm air on your feet. While driving, you marvel at how dark it is in this rural area, with no street lights to add to the car's headlights.

After about 15 minutes, you see something out of the corner of your eye; off to the right of your car, a dark shadow moves. Suddenly a tree crashes across the road behind you. You pull over and stop but the car continues moving on its own – shaking and vibrating. Trying to make sense of what is happening, you're startled when a tree drops right in front of you, missing your car by only a few feet.

You're in an earthquake.

When the shaking stops you see trees lying across the road ahead and behind you; your car is completely hemmed in. An aftershock hits; smaller branches and debris fall in and around the area.

It's getting darker.

What are you going to do? How safe will you be? How comfortable?

What is in your car?

CHAPTER 3

Options and Decisions

WHEN A DISASTER STRIKES and you're in your car away from home, there are some things you should consider and decisions you'll need to make. In some situations the conclusion will be simple: fallen power lines have started a fire nearby and you have to evacuate the area immediately. In others, you'll need to assess the situation fully, decide and then act. In every instance, you need to LOOK first, then use that information to choose your best option.

First and foremost is the decision to stay with your car or leave it. To answer that question, here are some things you might want to think about:

- Are you in danger – right now or in the next few hours?

- How far away from home or similar safe place are you?

- What is the time of day?

- What is the weather?

- Are there annoying pests or dangerous animals about?

- Is the route you need to take safe?

15

- What condition are you in? Tired? Scared to death?

- What is your health and fitness level? Are you ill? Is "hiking out" a possibility?

- What supplies do you have with you?

- Is there something you will soon need, necessitating a decision to leave?

If the best solution is to leave, you may wish to consider:

- How far will you have to walk? Can you make it in one day or will darkness force you to stop?

- If you will sleep outside, can you keep warm, dry?

- Do you have the clothing and shoes that will allow you to walk or hike out?

- Is visibility sufficient to enable you to avoid hazards?

If you decide to stay where you are, at least for now, consider:

- What do you have in your car?

- Will it be safer to stay inside your car or will you need to create a "campsite"?

- Does the situation allow for you to make a fire for warmth, heating food or as a signal?

Let's take a close look at each point above and think it through. Remember, the first decision to make is should you stay or leave?

Are you in danger – right now or in the next few hours?

- If buildings or trees have fallen around your car you could expect more of the same during aftershocks.

- Fallen power lines could spark and ignite brush in the area. Rising water or sliding mud could quickly pose real life and death situations.

If any such conditions exist, it's obvious: you need to grab survival items from your car and go. If your area seems safe from such dangers, you may want to stay put, get some rest and then plan your next move.

How far away from home or similar safe place are you?

- Take into consideration how far away from a better place you really are. Be realistic here: while you really want to be home with friends and family, don't underestimate how long it may take to get there. You don't know the condition of the road ahead – or behind. Will you be climbing over trees, buildings or boulders? Play it safe and have plenty of daylight to march out in.

- Take a moment and think of friends or fellow business owners you may know nearby. If you were able to get there, they might offer greater protection and comfort. Consider the terrain and neighborhood near their homes and offices. Think it through.

What is the time of day?

- Let's say it's 5:00 pm. In high summer, there may be nearly five hours of "daylight" left; in winter, you may

17

have only a few minutes. To walk out safely you need to see clearly as you make your way through potentially dangerous terrain.

What is the weather?

- You know your area and what the weather is like. Summer means blistering heat and humidity in one part of the country, cool, drizzling rain in another.

- Don't underestimate the effect heat, cold or moisture can have on your ability to survive. Sunstroke and hypothermia are real dangers.

Are there annoying pests or dangerous animals about?

- Walking home means one thing to someone living in the Pacific Northwest and something else to someone residing in Florida. The time of year is important too. Will you be coping with snakes or alligators? Could you stumble across a cougar or a mama bear with her cubs?

- Don't underestimate the maddening discomfort of dealing with 50,000 mosquitoes, chiggers, no-see-ums and gnats.

Is the route you need to take safe?

- Some people can walk through criminal-infested slums at midnight and emerge unscathed. Others are robbed or molested in the glaring sunshine of day. If you decide to walk out consider your route's potential dangers and plan accordingly.

What condition are you in? Tired? Scared to death?

- Take a moment and determine how you really feel. If you're coming off a twelve-hour work shift, now is not the time to begin a nine-mile hike. You'll make better decisions after you've rested.

- Adrenalin is a powerful hormone. Your body produces it in response to dangerous situations. This "fight or flight" substance increases heart rate so that more blood can be diverted to muscles. It can make you feel energized, shaky, weak or nauseated. An inability to think clearly can also occur. Whatever the symptoms, once adrenalin kicks in, it has to run its course, moving through your system before things get back to normal.

Understanding this beforehand can help tremendously. You won't worry that your pulse is racing or that you're feeling sick, but will recognize what's happening and wait for your body to return to normal.

In a disaster situation there's an excellent chance you'll experience an adrenalin rush. Your body is getting ready to run a mile or climb a tree – but what if you can't do either of those?

When the ground shook and buildings and trees fell, boy were you ready! But then things quieted down and there was nothing to do. You're left with an extreme case of the jitters and can't settle down.

You can help work it off by doing something physical like taking a walk, or if that isn't safe, move your arms and legs around, walk or jog in place. Drinking water also helps with the process.

- The body will stop creating adrenaline when the perceived danger is past. But what if the danger continues?

Prolonged stress will keep the body in a "ready" condition and that can cause actual physical, mental and emotional problems. Difficulty sleeping, stomach problems, impaired concentration and emotional flare-ups are common in an extended emergency situation.

What is your health and fitness level? Are you ill? Is "hiking out" a possibility?

- Being in the middle of a bout with pneumonia or having an arm in a cast will definitely limit your options.

- Your age, health and agility are factors to take into account, but consider carefully the decision to stay put. Is it real that someone will come looking for you? How long will your supplies last?

What supplies do you have with you?

- If you haven't prepared your car, you will soon have no other option than to hike out. A person can survive three minutes without oxygen, three hours without shelter, three days without water and three weeks without food. But keep in mind: toward the end of those hours, days and weeks, the body will be severely debilitated and incapable of much activity.

- Taking each of these in order, let's look at oxygen. When and how could you do anything about that? In fires or volcanic eruptions, the air may be so clogged with debris that breathing will be difficult. Toxic spills can also occur, making the air hazardous to breathe. Local hardware stores carry dust masks ($8) and toxic waste masks ($20+) to help filter the air.

- Shelter needs to be your second priority and experts say you have only hours to get out of the elements and get warm or cool and dry. That advice includes dry clothing! See Resources chapter for website on how to build emergency shelters.

  According to the Mayo Clinic, "Hypothermia is a medical emergency that occurs when your body loses heat faster than it can produce heat, causing a dangerously low body temperature." [1]

  Symptoms of hypothermia can begin with a lack of coordination and quickly escalate to confusion and an indifference to one's condition. Victims have been known to remove warm clothing and walk away from survival gear, to perish in the cold.

  Hyperthermia (heat exhaustion, sunstroke) can also generate confusion and occurs when the body generates or absorbs heat beyond its ability to cool.

- Water is very important to survival. A three day supply will be quickly used up. Whether you stay with your car or hike out, a major objective must be finding drinkable water.

- You can last weeks without food, but physical energy and mental acuity diminish rapidly along with your sense of well being.

  Whether for survival or comfort, having a well-stocked car will make a huge difference.

Is there something you will soon need, necessitating a decision to leave?

- Examples here would be food and water of course, but also medications you may need to take regularly.

How far will you have to walk? Can you make it in one day or will darkness force you to stop?

- Do you have the clothing and shoes that will allow you to walk or hike out?

- If you must sleep outside, can you keep warm, dry?

- You are literally dependent upon what you have with you. You won't get very far stumbling over fallen trees in high heels and if you don't have a coat to keep rain from soaking you, nighttime is going to be extremely uncomfortable or dangerous.

Is visibility sufficient to enable you to avoid hazards?

- You may decide to hike out only to find that your route is blocked in all directions. Mud, fallen trees and downed power lines can be deadly barriers.

- Having enough light to see pitfalls before you walk into them is crucial. The tools and equipment that you keep in your car could be the difference between life and death.

If you decide to stay with your car, what do you have in it?

- Can you stay warm? Do you have water and food? A flashlight? These are pretty basic necessities but they will determine the level of your survival and comfort.

Will it be safer to stay inside your car or will you want to create a "campsite"?

- If the threat of falling rocks, buildings or trees is a hazard, you may need to leave and find a safer place. A car's roof is no protection against large falling objects.

- Without heat or air conditioning, your car is nothing more than a metal box. It will soon get very cold or very hot depending on the weather.

- The length of time you'll be camping in your car will affect your options. A day or two is one thing; a week or two is quite another!

Does the situation allow for you to make a fire for warmth, heating food or as a signal?

- If possible, setting up a camp site may be a useful option. Nothing beats a warm meal at night and the glow from a campfire does more than heat the body and light up the night. It's quite a morale booster!

- Whether you want to let others know your location is something to think about too, and is dependent upon the type of disaster situation you are in. Listening to a radio could alert you to dangerous activity such as looting. Fellow travelers can be a real asset – or a real liability. Would you be safer not announcing your presence?

How prepared are you? What is in your car?

Reference:

[1] *http://www.mayoclinic.org/diseases-conditions/hypothermia/basics/definition/con-20020453*

CHAPTER 4

Scenarios: What Would You Do?

WEBSTER'S NEW WORLD DICTIONARY defines *scenario* as "an outline for any proposed or planned series of events, real or imagined."

In this chapter I'm going to invite you to play with a couple of disaster scenarios – and I do mean play. The more *serious* you are, the less capable you will be. If you're in a mind set where any small mistake results in terrible consequences, you're all the more likely to freeze. You want your mind free to create, create, create – solutions, solutions and even better solutions.

Now's the time to play with this information, when a "mistake" can be corrected simply by changing your mind.

Get comfortable with the concepts. When a disaster happens you'll already be mentally prepared and your actions will follow naturally.

In each scenario, decide whether you'll stay or leave. Determine what you'll do if you stay and what you'll take with you if you leave. The more details you put in the better.

Make it real.

25

Next chapter, I'll tell you what *my* actions would be for each scenario, providing another perspective of how to handle the "imagined series of events." If you have a friend who is interested, ask for *his* solutions. The more viewpoints you get the better.

Before you begin, please read these additional thoughts about why participating in these exercises could be important to you.

An emergency preparedness instructor once told my class that statistically, people who had prepared in advance were more likely to survive a major disaster. They were also more resilient once the emergency had passed.

The reason wasn't because they had disaster kits, it was because they'd thought through options *before* they were in danger. When the event happened, they were mentally prepared and made better decisions.

In addition, we were warned about a unique "hidden" danger of earthquakes, and it has to do with the way our minds work.

If you heard that a tornado was due in your area, your mind would be primed for it, just as it would be for a severe storm, flood or hurricane. With an earthquake there's no warning; we don't know when one's going to occur and when it does, the mind is stunned.

"*What* was that? *What* happened? *What* can I do about it?" The mind goes a little bit nuts. And just as it's recovering from such a rude insult, an aftershock occurs – *another* jolt it was totally unprepared for. At that point, the mind switches to overdrive, getting ready for more impacts.

With the mind so involved, earthquake victims can appear unresponsive or unable to deal with what's happening right now. They can't think – just at a time when they need to think.

We can minimize that effect by imagining an earthquake scenario in advance. Role playing – actually running through what it would be like, can help immensely. When an earthquake does happen, the mind is familiar with the concept and will react more quickly.

You will feel more confident in an emergency if you consider *now* what your actions should be *then*.

One more suggestion: take each scenario through to a *successful* solution. You're in the driver's seat after all. Success is what it's all about in surviving a disaster. Let's build some successful survival solutions.

Now on to the scenarios:

Scenario #1

You're at work when a fire truck pulls up in front of the building. The fireman knocks on the door and announces you have ten minutes to evacuate the area. A wildfire burning miles away is now out of control and everyone within ten square miles has to leave.

The route to your home lies directly in the path of the closed off area. You will need to drive away using different roads.

- What will you do with those ten minutes?

- What will you toss into your car? You only have ten minutes.

- Where will you go? You'll be at least ten miles away from both home and work.

- There might be lots of cars on the road, evacuating just as you are. Do you have enough gas? Will you find a motel?

- What resources do you have with you?

What is in your car already?

Scenario #2

It's 4:00 pm on a wonderfully sunny day following a week of steady rain. You've spent the day hiking up a moderately difficult trail and have just returned to the trailhead where the car is parked. You're ready to drive home, thinking a stop off for pizza might be in order.

As you leave the parking area, you feel a rumbling vibration followed by tremendous cracking sounds. You begin a left turn only to see a huge landslide now blocking the road.

You turn the car in the opposite direction and head out. The road is clear and there's no indication more mud and trees will fall, but you keep driving past several trailheads, wanting to put as much distance between you and the slide as possible.

Finally you stop your car, get out and listen. No more ominous sounds, but you're also driving in a direction and on a road you're not familiar with. Pulling out the hiking guide you'd purchased at the district's ranger station, you discover that access to the major roadway has been blocked by the slide.

What will you do?

- Will you continue driving or park for the night? It won't be long before dark. You won't be able to see hazards in the road nor will you be able to easily make camp if you wait much longer.

- What supplies do you have with you?

- Do you have contact information with you so you can call friends and family to let them know your situation?

- How safe will you be? How comfortable?

Here and now, in the comfort of wherever you're reading this book, go through the options from chapter three and make your decisions.

If you make the situation real and think it through, you'll discover what you'd need and what you should do.

What is in your car?

A Disaster Preparedness Guide by DJ Castle

Notes

CHAPTER 5

What I Would Do

IN EACH OF THE PRECEDING SCENARIOS you needed to make decisions. Those decisions aren't set in stone; you can always change your mind, but you need a starting point. Check your solutions with mine as I describe what I would do.

Scenario #1: You weren't given an option whether to stay or leave in this one – you had to leave. This year we've seen many instances of people being forced to evacuate their homes quickly due to fires or floods. It does happen.

The pre-planning I've done guarantees that everything I'll need for immediate survival is *already packed in my car*. Water, food, clothing, prescriptions – it's all in my car's trunk, waiting to be used. So if ordered to evacuate, I can focus on loading pets in the car and gathering irreplaceable files and documents that are important to my work or home life.

Those items have also been pre-selected and are ready to be scooped up. A checklist ensures I won't miss a single object or action and I've rehearsed the scene, going through all the motions right up to getting out – in just ten minutes.

While we aren't going to discuss home evacuation here, one piece of information needs to be in your car right now: proof of residency or ownership. Local authorities and FEMA will require that documentation – and if your house or apartment building is no longer there, it will be difficult to get. Make a copy of an electric or mortgage bill right now and put it in your car.

The website and videos that inspired me to prepare for a home evacuation in advance are available at The Insurance Information Institute: *http://www.iii.org*. The Youtube video was uploaded on September 24, 2007: *http://www.youtube.com/watch?v=TLtrntXifkY*

One video is called "The Ten Minute Challenge" and portrays two families being given ten minutes to leave their homes. Both households have children and pets – the difference is in their reaction to the situation.

The adults of one family have prepared extensively for such an emergency. Mom and Dad have separate tasks to accomplish and immediately set about doing them. The other family has never even considered the concept – and it shows. They rush around trying to decide what to take and finally leave with little or nothing of importance.

It's quite an eye-opener.

This year, wildfires alone forced thousands to evacuate. Many people left with nothing and had nothing to return to.

Evacuating from home is an important subject, and made a lot easier when most of what you need is already in your car.

Wherever you are, you're always near your car.

Scenario #2: I would choose to stay and would want to select a place while there was still light. Driving away from the dangerous area, I'd bear in mind that trailhead parking areas are usually flat and have the luxury of portable toilets. They often have a gravel surface which would allow me to hear the approach of someone – by car or on foot, in advance. I'd look for a good trailhead parking lot.

While I don't know much about mudslides, I'd study the terrain of the trailhead, perhaps choosing a site away from the side of a steep hillside.

The hiking area described here can have a phone reception problem, so I'd try calling from multiple locations before parking for the night. In this case I wouldn't expect cell phone lines to be jammed (as they would likely be in an earthquake), so I'd try reaching a neighbor who might have information on what just happened. He could pass on my identity and location to authorities who might later come to the scene. I'd also listen to the car radio before parking the car for the night.

I'd use the remaining daylight to walk about the site, familiarizing myself with the land, foliage and where that toilet is! I'd also be listening, alert for signs of additional slides or other dangers and generally getting used to the sounds in my area.

Knowing that my car and I are quite prepared to stay overnight in this situation, I'd begin moving items from my trunk to the interior.

First I'd set up lighting: I wouldn't want to use the interior lights for long, so I'd unpack the two lanterns I carry: one is battery-operated fluorescent and the other is solar charged LED.

Next I'd set up my sleeping area, unrolling my sleeping bag onto the back seat, placing some items within easy reach of the "bed": a bottle of water, tissues, one of the lanterns and a flashlight.

Carrying my survival backpack from the trunk to the front passenger seat, I'd pull out the things I'd need to set up a washing station outside the car with a gallon jug of water, soap, wash cloth and towel. I'd unpack a roll of toilet paper – just in case, and put my sleepwear (sweat pants and shirt) on the sleeping bag. Dinner would be something I could eat right from can or pouch – it's all in there because I put it there, knowing what I'd want in an emergency.

Individual needs and preferences vary which is why I encourage you to determine what *you* will need.

I'll give a personal example here: I wear contact lenses and need to remove them at night. For that operation I'd need clean hands and plenty of light. Lens solutions and storage case are all in my kit and since I can't see very far without contacts, I'd position prescription glasses near the bed.

In this situation I'm not in danger and have familiar, useful items to help me feel as comfortable as possible.

When it's time to turn in, I'll take a final trip to that outhouse, wash hands, change into a comfortable sweat suit, snuggle into my sleeping bag and listen to the quiet of the forest.

I've got what I need in my car.

CHAPTER 6

What To Get And How To Store It All In Your Car

I PROMISED THIS WASN'T GOING TO BE a book of lists. There are websites and pamphlets galore listing hundreds of items for you to put into your disaster kit. I've given a few websites in the "Resources" chapter.

You know what you need – you're already using it! And from toothbrush to hand soap, these are the same items you'll be needing when living out of a car or hiking home.

WHEN should you make a kit? *Right Now.* Envision yourself in one of the scenarios I've given, put this book down and gather some things together to fit that situation. Put everything in a box or a bag and put it in the trunk. Now! Tonight! You'll be that much closer to being prepared.

Once you have *something* in place, you can always improve upon it. Write down what you'll need, then review some of the prepared lists I mentioned. They will jog your memory and cause you to think of other items.

In each scenario, light has been an important consideration. Imagine what it would be like to be in absolute darkness with nothing to light your way – not fun; not safe. Oil or kerosene lamps just aren't compatible with cars. Obtaining a battery-operated fluorescent or LED lantern and a couple of

35

flashlights would be the safest course. Check out the "Resources" chapter later on in the book.

Water is crucial. Buy at least one gallon jug at the store and put it in your car right now. It's more important to have water on hand than food.

Can you find sources of water in your area – a pond or stream? If so, then a filtration water bottle might be ideal. You scoop up some water, squeeze it through the built-in filter and it comes out filtered or purified. If you're in dry, desert country, you'd just better pack more water.

Think through what you will need in the terrain you're most likely to get stuck in – with only your car and what it contains.

What would you eat -- right from the can or box? No preparation, no heating, just grab and eat. In a disaster you won't have time or energy to cook. Find the foods you like – enough to eat for at least three days, and put them in the car. You can buy cans with pop tops, pouches that have tear off tops – you won't even need a can opener. Put something to eat in your car.

HOW you go about getting the survival items you need depends on your time and budget. It's kind of fun to go on a shopping spree, buying specialty products at camping supply stores and grocery stores have an aisle that offers sample bottles of everything from soap to hand cream.

If you can't justify buying new things just to put into a car kit, here's another way: don't buy new, REPLACE. Isn't it time you got a new toothbrush? Dentists tell us we should get new ones every three months. Well, this time take the old one, douse it with hydrogen peroxide to kill any germs and after it's dry, put it into a zip plastic bag. Grab a toothpaste tube that's half gone...and dental floss, hand soap, and...pretty soon everything you need will be accounted for. In all cases, what you pack will be determined by the potential nature of the emergency and where you live.

If the situation is truly a major disaster, you won't be able to find even basic necessities for a long time. No ATM machines or cash registers will be working, so if a store does have some supplies, you'll need exact change. Be sure to include some money in your kit – small bills and coins.

Car trunks vary in size, and some cars don't even have trunks! You'll need to come up with a solution for that, but there's quite a bit of room in any car if you look for it. All those nooks and crannies can store valuable life-supporting items.

My Toyota Camry has a very small trunk compared to other Camrys, because it's a Hybrid and the batteries take up most of the space. But there's still a lot of room for my survival gear.

Consider your car's trunk as a small room that is waiting to be stocked with the special items you will need for survival and comfort.

Empty trunk of my Toyota Hybrid

What should you pack your emergency supplies in? There's no hard and fast rule, you just won't want to search through the entire car for a protein bar or a flashlight. You'll want all your gear in one place – and if disaster conditions demand that you hike out, you'll need something to carry it all in.

Duffels, satchels, backpacks, handbags, briefcases – there are dozens of carryalls out there to choose from.

Personally I like backpacks. When hiking, they leave my hands free and many have outside pockets. I like lots of outer pockets: that's where I stash important "grab-it-now" stuff. Flashlight, whistle, compass, multi-tool – these items could be needed quickly and are just an unzip away.

You can pay $6 to well over $1000 for a backpack. Make sure your selection is relevant to what you need. Perhaps you already have one that hasn't been used for awhile. Does your nephew have one he's going to toss? Has your daughter outgrown her school backpack?

Thrift stores often have bins full of them. I bought one recently that looked brand new. I wiped it down, sprayed it with vinegar, let it air in the sun and it was good to go. (And it has **lots** of outside pockets!)

Look for a pack large enough to hold what you will need for a minimum of three days.

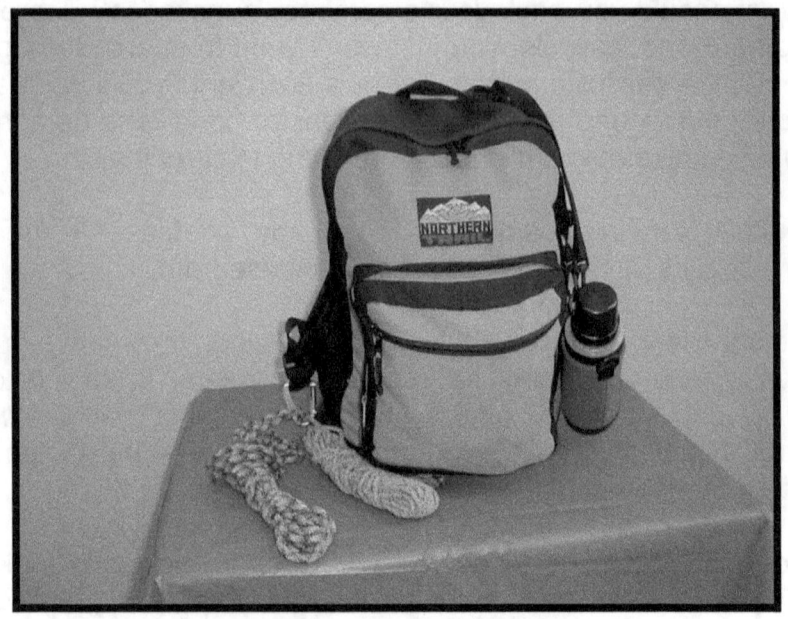

Basic Three-Day Pack

I've had several different packs in my car over the years and a couple of problems kept coming up. Time would go by and I'd wonder if I'd packed a certain item – and would end up dumping out the entire contents searching for it.

The problem was solved by typing up a master inventory of every single thing in the pack and saving it to the computer. Listing items by their location, like "outer right pocket" or "main body" allows me to locate an item quickly. A copy of the list now resides inside a zip plastic bag, tucked into an easy-to-reach backpack pocket. I review my kit seasonally, exchanging winter gloves for sunscreen and replacing any foods or products that have expired.

I know what I have in my car.

Another problem I've had is deciding just how extensive my kit should be. For instance, I own several camping stoves, each with its own type of fuel. And there are some tasty meals made for hikers that are prepared by just adding boiling water – they'd be very welcome in winter time.

But add a stove and you need cans or sticks of fuel, and then a cook pot and…finally the kit becomes too heavy to carry.

And what if I were downtown when an emergency hit? I might have to stay in a shelter for a few nights and probably wouldn't be allowed to use that sort of gear.

Will I need to hike home? Will I have to stay in my car overnight or for two weeks? The type of emergency or disaster dictates how extensive a kit should be and we just don't have that information in advance!

My solution was to create an extra pack. This kit holds camp stoves, fuel, water purifier and extra food. When an emergency happens I'll have the option of selecting what's needed from the "extras" in this second pack.

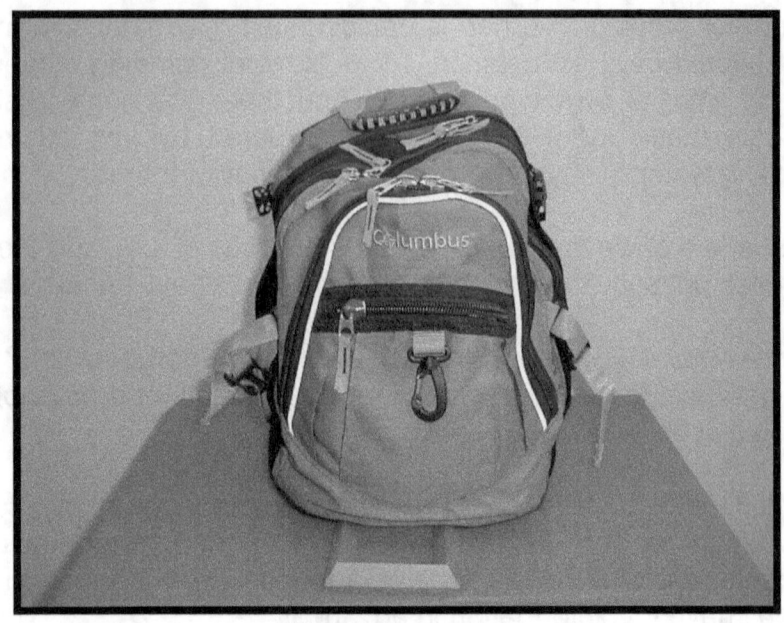

Extra Pack

Each kit has its own inventory page and on the back is a list of contents of *all* the packs in my car. When an emergency happens, I can easily pick and choose, taking only what is needed for the situation.

My car's trunk also holds some camping items that may not be applicable to you. Storing a hatchet or a camp shovel in *your* trunk may not make a lot of sense if you live in downtown Los Angeles, but they'd be considered standard equipment in more rural areas.

Pack what *you* need and want.

Here's an exercise I hope you'll try. Go out and sit in your car. Don't turn the engine on – just sit, and imagine you have to live there for several days.

Look around. How would you set things up? What would you need to have? What would you *like* to have?

Then answer the question, *where could I put those items?*

Prepare right now, because wherever you are, you're always near your car.

Notes

CHAPTER 7

Earthquake!

PLACE YOURSELF in this disaster scenario. What you would do? Could you do as well as these folks? Would you handle things differently?

You're working late at your office in town. The rest of the staff went home hours ago; you're finishing a computer report when a major earthquake shakes your building. All the lights flicker and go out. Light fixtures and ceiling tiles begin falling from the ceiling.

You duck under the desk, grabbing onto its legs as the shaking continues. When it stops, you stay where you are, waiting for any aftershocks.

It is very dark; no street lights shine through the office windows. Before anything, you realize, you must have light.

Remembering there's a flashlight in the desk drawer, you move toward it; reaching upward, your hand touches only jagged pieces of metal leaning against the right side of the desk.

You're beginning to feel frightened, thinking you might be trapped. Taking a few deep breaths, you try to think of any other lighting sources nearby. Ah yes, there's a small flashlight on your key chain – in the drawer on the other side of the desk.

Crawling forward, you find that drawer and are able to tug it open and grab the keys. Turning the small flashlight on, you point it in all directions.

The metal you felt is actually a filing cabinet that used to be against the wall behind you. It's now lodged against most of the desk, but there is a small open area and you move toward it.

An aftershock hits and you scramble back, holding the flashlight near your body to protect it. Debris falls from the ceiling, but this is a lighter jolt and only lasts a few seconds.

The aftershock actually helped your situation, moving the filing cabinet a few inches, allowing you to open the desk drawer and remove the larger flashlight. What a difference! Now you can sweep the room with the light and see where to walk and how to escape.

For escape you must. There's no one else in the building, no reason to remain – except for one thing: your building has a natural gas furnace. As if your thought triggered the event, you notice a slight gas smell.

Participation in the office's emergency drills is paying off: you know where the gas valve is, how to turn it off and that the tool needed is located nearby. Your light shows minimal debris; you carefully make your way to the furnace and can indeed smell gas. As you have practiced, you touch the wall before reaching for the metal tool, ensuring that any static electricity is discharged and moving slowly so as not to generate a spark, you turn the valve to the off position.

It's time to leave.

You manage to maneuver through the office toward the exit, bracing for what you might see outside. You hear distant sirens but know that any help for this area will be a long time coming.

The exit door deadbolt moves easily, allowing you to step outside. It's pitch black and your flashlight shows building after building damaged by the quake. Some appear partially collapsed and you wonder if anyone was inside. Your car, parked on the street in front, seems to be undamaged.

Mentally sorting through the six office buildings on your block, you realize there actually might be people in some of them – especially the business next to yours, a tax preparation firm. You've had lunch with the owners, Steve and Shirley, a few times and remember they often work as late as this.

Walking toward their building, you shine the light along its walls all the way up to the roof: there appears to be minimal structural damage. The front door is locked but a window near it is broken out and shining your light through it, you call Shirley's name.

"Are you in there? Is anyone in there?"

"Yes, I'm here!"

You recognize Shirley's voice.

"Are you ok?"

"I'm not hurt but there's furniture here blocking the door and I can't get past it!"

"Ok. I'm coming to help."

Just then a figure comes running down the street, flashlight in hand. You recognize Steve, Shirley's husband, wearing a safety vest, backpack and hard hat.

He asks, *"Are you all right? Have you seen Shirley? She's working tonight!"*

"She's ok, Steve, she just told me she's not hurt, but can't get out the door. Let's go see."

Steve unlocks the front door and you both enter the building, directing your flashlight beams around the room.

"Shirley, where are you?" yells Steve.

"I'm back near the break room! The table is blocking the door."

"Ok, we're coming!"

Moving slowly toward the sound of Shirley's voice, you and Steve reach her location and see that indeed, a heavy worktable is jammed against the entry way. It takes all three of you to push and pull it free, but eventually Shirley is able to get out of the room.

Shining his flashlight over her body, Steve says *"It looks like you're ok. Let's get out of here."*

"Fine by me," Shirley says shakily.

"Wait a sec, Shirley, does your office have gas?" you ask.

"No, we're all electric," replies Shirley.

"Great! Let's go!"

Moving around the debris, you exit the building; Steve and Shirley hug and both reach out to you; all are grateful to be safe and alive.

The three of you begin discussing what to do next. According to Shirley, it's unlikely that there are workers in neighboring businesses, but you're reluctant to leave without making sure.

Before continuing, Steve pulls a permanent marking pen from his pack and draws an "X" on the wall next to the office door. He writes his initials, the time, date and a zero in the space, turns to us and explains.

"These symbols will tell emergency personnel that we've searched the buildings, and that no one is inside."

After asking me questions about my building, he puts the same design on its door, adding "Gas Off" to the drawing.

The three of you walk up the block listening, shouting into the structures, alert for any gas odors. The buildings are empty and Steve draws the "all clear" symbol near each door.

You're all tired. There haven't been any more aftershocks; Steve suggests heading to their house which is a couple of blocks away.

"The house wasn't damaged much, Shirley. It seemed ok."

"Come on," she says. *"Let's all go home."*

You ask, *"Steve, are the roads drivable?"*

"Not the way I came," he says. *"Let's wait 'til tomorrow to get your car."*

"Ok, let me grab some stuff from the trunk. Could you help me carry a few things?"

"Of course. We'll put you in the guest room or if it's too damaged, we have a couch."

"Sounds wonderful. I really appreciate…"

"We're all in this together," Shirley says and gives you a hug.

Walking down the block, you see a few young men walking toward you; one is carrying a kerosene lantern.

"We're searching buildings. Are you ok?" he asks.

Steve recognizes a neighbor's son and gives details on the nearby buildings. The men had checked out houses in their own neighborhood and planned to continue their search. You inform them that there are natural gas lines in the area. The young man thanks you and immediately blows out his lantern.

At the house, the three of you walk around the building and through the house, checking for any danger, and then make your way to the kitchen. Steve sets a lantern on the table and you gratefully sink into chairs. It's been a busy few hours.

They turn on a portable radio, learning that the quake damage is quite widespread. There is no electricity in the neighborhood and fires are burning in some places.

Realizing you should let loved ones know that you're alive and unhurt, you call an out-of-state contact. He has messages for you as well: your friends and family are uninjured and he promises to call them back, letting them know you won't be home tonight, but that you're safe.

You've been pretty lucky so far: you're not hurt, you're not alone, people you know have invited you to stay at their house....

What kind of a guest will you be?

If I were the "you" in this story, I'd be a very good guest indeed. Let's go back to that final visit to your car before walking to the house with Steve and Shirley. Here's how it would go if it were my car:

"Could you help me carry a few things?"

"Of course. We'll put you in the guest room or if it's too damaged, we have a couch."

"Sounds wonderful. I really appreciate..."

"We're all in this together," Shirley says and gives me a hug.

In a very short time, I take items from trunk and glove compartment, setting them next to the car: sleeping bag, my three-day disaster pack, a gallon of water, another mini-flashlight and two battery-operated lanterns.

I leave the extra pack behind. If we need my cooking gear or tools, we'll get them tomorrow. For tonight I'm all set. I won't need to impose on my hosts at all: from water to food to personal hygiene, I have all I need. In fact I have extra.

"Shirley, Steve how are you guys on water? I have a couple gallons here."

"We're good for tonight, but thanks for offering. Ready? Let's go, it's not far."

What would *you* have to take along to Steve and Shirley's house?

What's in your car?

CHAPTER 8

The First Night ... And Then What?

L ET'S RETURN TO STEVE AND SHIRLEY'S house. Back at the kitchen table, you share thoughts and information: no lights, no running water and the plumbing is suspect.

Hmmm, no water, no toilet; this could be awkward.

Hopefully Steve and Shirley have a plan for the "no plumbing problem". If I'm in the scenario, I have a nifty product in my pack created by a company called Cleanwaste®. They market portable bathroom units and supplies and I have several of the plastic bags and powder in my kit. (See chapter nine for product information.)

It's been a hectic night; we prepare sleeping areas and say goodnight.

Morning dawns: you've unexpectedly slept like a log. You're in a strange house with people you barely know, and the day will bring heaven knows how many new challenges. As the day progresses, you start considering options: should you stay or leave?

The answer will depend upon the nature and extent of the earthquake damage. It could take quite awhile before streets are cleared enough to allow you to drive home. As time goes by and conditions change, you'll continue to evaluate your decision to stay or leave.

"We're all in this together," Shirley had said when she invited you to stay at her house.

But just how long will this emergency last?

Remember those bridges I talked about in the first chapter? One county estimated that of its eight major bridges, four would likely collapse following a 9.0 earthquake. They also declared that a partial restoration of just one major Interstate would take six to twelve months. [1]

Six months? A year?

You might have heard that following a disaster, we should expect to be on our own for three days. Sensible preppers know that one to two *weeks* is more realistic.

If you cannot get home, you will have exactly what's on your back and in your car.

How long will you be able to camp out at Shirley's house? How prepared are *they*? If roads are impassable, how will delivery trucks transport food to the supermarkets in their neighborhood?

Put yourself in Steve and Shirley's shoes: how long could *you* host someone in such an emergency? How stocked is *your* pantry? How much water do *you* have stored? How many "guests" could *you* help and for how long?

Those questions need to be answered from a household-preparedness perspective, which is beyond the scope of this guide – but please consider them!

Back to Shirley's house:

Eventually, hopefully, you'll work out a plan for returning to your own residence. In this situation, these are the items to consider before you leave:

- Is the entire route to your home cleared for driving? If not, can you expect that it soon will be?

- What alternative routes could you take?

- Will you have to walk? Could you?

- Will water be available along your route?

- Are there "safe havens" along the way you could use to make the trip possible?

As we take a closer look at each of these considerations, make note of the supplies you'd like to have in your car for such a disaster.

The route: if you have a portable radio you can learn which roads and bridges are damaged and closed to traffic.

Alternative routes: with maps you can plot different routes and if you needed to maneuver around obstacles or road closures, a GPS unit would be useful.

On foot: a hand-held GPS – the kind hikers use, would likewise help you re-route the path as you go.

It is imperative that you have access to drinking water. Whether you're traveling by car or on foot, you must locate or carry sufficient water in order to survive.

Safe havens: whether you're walking or driving, circumstances could prevent you from making the trip in one day. It would help a great deal if you knew people who lived along the route you intend to take. If road conditions deteriorated or darkness fell and you knew a friend lived nearby, you could consider staying there overnight. Or perhaps you could leave your car there and hike the rest of the way home.

In my pack is a contact list of friends, fellow business owners and acquaintances I consider safe haven potential. It was compiled by reviewing where I drive on a weekly or monthly basis. The information is assembled by city, with phone numbers, addresses and a mileage estimate to each friend's home or office. Whether they live just a mile down the road or twenty miles away, I have their contact information with me on a two-sided piece of paper. (See example at the end of this chapter.)

At the bottom of the list I add the names and phone numbers of doctors as well as out-of-state contacts. This list goes into each survival pack I carry.

Now, who do you know who lives along roads *you* travel frequently? Relatives, church members, your hair dresser or dentist – these are people who would likely help if you were in their vicinity. You may need that assistance in a disaster situation.

Why should you create such a list in advance? Remember the effect an earthquake can have on a person's mind? What state will *your* mind and memory be in after you've gone through a major catastrophe?

I strongly suggest you create such a list and put copies in your car and by your phones at home and work.

Reference:

[1]*http://www.oregonlive.com/portland/index.ssf/2014/02/earthquake_planning_in_multnom.html*

Example

Side One: Safe Haven Contacts

Put your own name, address and all of your phone numbers here.

Phone Numbers
Lake City
Sally Smith   (423) 333-3333 cell, 222-2222 work
Bill Jones   (335) 555-5555 home, 333-3331 cell
Rick Hall   (322) 222-2222 cell, 233-3333 home

Canyon City
Tanya Jones   (335) 550-0000 cell 299-9999 work
Dick Smith   (329) 555-5555 cell, 333-3222 work

Doctors
Pat Jones, DC   (312) 555-1111
Dale Smith, MD   (410) 555-5555
Peter James, DDS (220) 333-1111

Out of State Contacts
List several people living in other states who will act as relay points between you and loved ones when local phone lines are damaged or jammed. This is the best way to get messages to and from people you need to reach. Make sure you get their agreement to be on this list and that they know what to do.

Example

Side Two: Safe Haven Directions

Address / Directions / [Mileage

Lake City
Sally Smith   5205 91st Ave NE
→Left Hwy 9 S, Right 4th St, Left 91st Ave NE   [5 miles]

Bill Jones   6602 32nd PL
→From Hwy 12, Right127th, Left 32nd PL [14 miles]

Rick Hall   3321 14th St. SW
→Right 3rd Ave, Left 14th St SW   [1 mile]

Canyon City
Tanya Jones 3012 42nd St
→Left Pike St, Right Hwy 3 S, Right 42nd St [3 miles]

Dick Smith   6602 3rd St
→Left 20th, Right Parkway Plaza, Left 3rd St [2 miles]

How prepared are you?

What's in your car?

Notes

CHAPTER 9

Why Didn't You Go Before We Left?

YOU GOT OUT OF WORK and headed for the car, anxious to get home. You hit the freeway...and five miles down the road, there's trouble. All cars slow down, then stop – and the highway becomes a parking lot. According to the radio, there's been a multiple car, injury accident on the road ahead and it's blocking all lanes.

It happens to commuters all the time. A usual drive home turns into something quite unusual. An hour passes, then two...and you have to "go to the bathroom".

This challenge needs to be part of your car preparedness project. In an emergency or disaster situation, you will need to have a solution, so prepare for it now, while you have the leisure to do so, before it becomes a necessity.

One approach is to purchase a fold-up, portable toilet, small enough to fit in a car. You can find them online or at camping and outdoor equipment stores for under $50; many come with plastic bags and a powder to control odor.

Another product is a toilet seat designed to clip onto an ordinary 5-gallon bucket. A plastic garbage bag lines the bucket, the seat snaps onto the top and you're set. While a bucket is a bit large to fit into your trunk, it could also serve as storage for other supplies, or a gallon jug of water. (Consider adding a lid for the bucket as well.)

Next, what do you do with the waste? Human feces must be handled in a specific manner or disease conditions can develop.

While researching this problem, I discovered a product created by Cleanwaste®. According to a company representative, "Poo Powder® is comprised of three main ingredients, a decay catalyst, a deodorizer and the NASA developed super absorbent which gels and deodorizes liquid and solid human waste on contact in less than 10 seconds." The material "can then be discarded into the trash." The powder can be ordered alone or with a portable toilet. View their website and demos:
http://www.cleanwaste.com/poo-powder-waste-treatment.

When an emergency traps you in your car for hours or days, you will need to handle your body's waste products.

Prepare now; you'll be very glad you did.

CHAPTER 10

Wash Your Hands!

E VERY CLASS I'VE ATTENDED has hammered home one point: in an emergency, disaster, or survival situation, sanitation is extremely important. You need to have a way to wash your hands.

Disposable wipes and hand sanitizers are very popular these days but according to the FDA, many companies are making unproven claims, promoting their products as preventing infection and disease. Evidence is also growing that the chemicals they contain can have negative health effects and we shouldn't be using them all the time.

You can get more information on this by doing a computer search for "chemicals in disposable hand wipes". Some websites offer safer substitutes and formulas for making your own hand sanitizer using common, household ingredients.

In a disaster situation this makes for quite a balancing act: chemicals or dirty hands?

If you have access to water, there's always soap! Washing hands for 20 seconds is the rule – and not necessarily in hot water either. The temperature required for killing germs and microorganisms is a lot higher than anyone could stand on their skin. Many authorities state that water, soap and friction are all you need to clean your hands.

The technique for washing your hands is pretty simple: wet your hands, apply enough soap to create a good lather, rub all parts of your hands and wrists for 20 seconds – outside the stream of water, then rinse and dry thoroughly.

When I did a lot of camping, I used a product called – guess what, Camp Soap. I looked for it online and it's still around, available at sporting goods stores and online. The website product summary states that Camp Soap:

> *"Effectively cleans anything washable in all water types and temperatures. Great for greasy pots, pans, dishes, utensils, clothing, packs, tents. And well suited for use on hands, face, body, hair. Free rinsing and environmentally compatible. It is Non-Toxic, PH Balanced, Hypo-Allergenic, Biodegradable, Fast acting, Phosphate Free. It is concentrated: use a small amount."*

There are many choices these days. The bottom line is: find something you can use in an emergency situation and put it in your car.

A valuable lesson I learned in the CERT course was to use disposable gloves. Our focus in that class was working with injured people who were bleeding, but gloves will also keep your hands clean when doing any dirty work.

A hot tip from one instructor was to put two pairs of gloves on your hands at the beginning of a task or project. When the outer pair becomes soiled, remove them and put a clean pair on over the first pair. It's easier than trying to put fresh gloves on sweaty hands!

A CPR class taught an effective way to remove contaminated gloves. You grasp one glove at the palm and pull it toward the fingers, gradually turning the glove inside out. You then gather that soiled glove in your other hand. Without touching the outside of the glove, slide your bare index finger inside the wrist band of your gloved hand, and pull that dirty glove outwards and down, inverting the glove trapping the first glove inside.

Thinking through emergency situations before they happen can be extremely valuable.

Determining what you may need in an emergency is vital.

What is in your car?

Notes

CHAPTER 11

Resources & Tips
Things That Work For Me

WHEN IT COMES TO STORING LEAKABLES in your emergency kit, zip plastic bags are your very best friend. Having shampoo or toothpaste all over everything won't be fun, so seal things up tight – and that includes canned food with pop tops!

Consider storing gallon jugs of water in your car instead of smaller bottles. Why? Try carrying a gallon's worth of those little bottles! When hiking out, the backpack leaves one hand free to grab a gallon jug – you'll have water.

When storing water in my car I always go overboard with packaging materials. The gallon jug goes inside a plastic bag, then into a tight-fitting cardboard box which is then put into another, larger plastic bag. It's probably overkill, but if that bottle leaks, my trunk *and its contents* will stay dry. I'll also be able to use those bags for other jobs when they're no longer needed as packing material.

Although bottled water doesn't "go bad", the plastic bottles can. They begin leaching chemicals into the water – that's what the expiration date is all about. It's wise to rotate your supplies.

You can only carry so much water with you – in your car or on your back; water filtration bottles could be invaluable in an emergency situation. Many filter out protozoa and bacteria down to 0.1 microns. Your favorite hiking or camping store should have several to choose from or search online using "water filtration bottle".

If you are in a survival situation for a long time, there are methods of extracting water from the ground and from plants that may be useful to learn. You can even make salt water drinkable. Here are a few websites:

http://www.wikihow.com/Make-Water-in-the-Desert

http://www.desertusa.com/mag98/dec/stories/water.html

http://www.instructables.com/id/Extract-Clean-Drinkable-Water-From-Plants/

https://www.youtube.com/watch?v=avZtD4gkM84

Mosquitoes can be a big problem where I live, so having a small container of repellant in my pack is a must. "CedarCide" is completely organic and can be purchased by the gallon or in small, ounce-sized containers through the website *http://www.cedarcide.com*. Mosquito netting is good to have and a "mosquito head net" will protect head, face and shoulders when walking about – very lightweight and worth every penny.

When you're without electricity, a source of light is vital. Fluorescent lanterns eliminate the hazards of an open flame, with many providing enough light to read by.

At a surplus store I came across a solar LED lamp called Luci Light. Made of clear, flexible, plastic material, it measures 5" in diameter, weighs only 4 ounces, inflates to 4" high and collapses to 1". According to the website, "Luci has three main components that make her work: a solar panel that captures photons from sunlight or incandescent light; a rechargeable internal battery that stores her power; and 10 LED bulbs that produce her light." When fully charged, the lamp is supposed to provide 6-12 hours of light – and mine lived up to that promise! The current website cost is $14.99. *https://www.mpowerd.com.*

In chapter nine I discussed managing human waste when plumbing isn't available. Go to *http://www.cleanwaste.com* for a variety of toilet kits and portable bathroom systems.

For cleaning up, there's a compressed cloth called a "1-2-3 Towel" that is handy. Each tiny towel is separately wrapped in cellophane and comes completely dehydrated. Due to its small size, several would easily fit into pack or glove box. When a small amount of water is placed on it, the towel expands to about 8"x12". The website says it's 100% natural, no additives. The best price I've found is online at *http://www.safaristraps.com* where you can get a package of ten for $2.50. They're also available at local sporting goods stores.

Cooking stoves each require their own type of fuel, but there's a portable wood stove that makes do with "twigs and scrap wood which are abundant and free, and it uses very little to get the job done." Made in the USA, the EmberLit Stove "weighs less than 11.3 oz, is constructed of stainless steel and packs flat." I've used it and consider it to be a valuable, light-weight addition to my pack. The website lists its current cost at $45 (*http://www.emberlit.com/en/emberlit-stove-stainless-steel*).

If you end up hiking away from your car, creating some sort of shelter could be necessary. That's where tarps and rope come in handy. There are great pictures and instructions for building emergency shelters at: *http://www.wilderness-survival.net/shelters-2.php*

Food selection tip: hikers know to hang their food pouches in trees away from their sleeping areas to prevent attracting bears and other hungry critters. And you probably won't want to be munching on smelly tuna fish or sardines when such an animal crosses your path. Don't laugh! They've been spotted in urban areas like Los Angeles and after a disaster they could be confused and very hungry.

Do you wear corrective lenses? An extra pair could be priceless in a disaster. For inexpensive glasses, try *http://www.cheapglasses.com*.

Decision Making

Years ago, while flying across the country, I listened to an audio book on the plane's headset channels. It so impressed me I purchased both audio cassette and book the moment I arrived home. *"Yes or No, The Guide to Better Decisions"* by Spencer Johnson, MD is a useful, interesting book. Told in story form, it follows a young man who is learning a better way to make decisions. I found the audiotape format suited me best. While listening to the information, my mind was free to roam through life decisions, focusing on areas that needed further attention using the "Yes or No" techniques.

Disaster and emergency situations require the ability to make yes or no decisions – often immediate ones. The book (and used versions of the audiocassette) can be found online using your computer's search engine.

Deals Deals Deals

Along the way I've learned where to get some unique items or products at less than full price.

- If you have a Harbor Freight in your area you'll be able to stock up on flashlights at the very best price – free, and they come *with batteries!* The store regularly advertises these mini flashlights in local newspapers, and you can register to receive their fliers by mail. *http://www.harborfreight.com.*

- Inexpensive batteries are also Harbor Freight items.

- *Http://www.cheaperthandirt.com* often has items from first aid kits to bungee cords at bargain rates.

Gadgets To Make Your Car Even More Valuable

- Most everyone knows you can charge your cell phone by plugging it into a car's cigarette lighter or power port. Did you know your car can also run household appliances? All you need is an "inverter".

The power that comes from a car battery is different than what is supplied to your house. A power inverter converts car battery power (DC) to household AC power, allowing you to plug in a two or three prong appliance.

The inverter can plug into the power port if less than 400 watts is needed. Higher wattage requires that it be attached to the car's battery by clips similar to a set of jumper cables. You'll need to know how many watts your device requires: while a typical clock radio uses only 10 watts, a hair dryer uses a minimum of 1200![1]

- Did you know that Ham Radios are available that can be used in your car? You may wish to learn more about this topic. Ham radio operators regularly help out in disaster situations, especially when cell phones are unreliable. They know what's happening right at the scene, hearing information that most of us won't get.

Caution!

A special note here about keeping warm: **don't** run your car's engine in order to use the heater. "Carbon monoxide (CO), an odorless, colorless gas, which can cause sudden illness and death, is produced any time a fossil fuel is burned."[2]

You won't know if you're a victim of CO poisoning until it's far too late. Prepare other ways of staying warm in or near your car.

Disaster Supplies Kit Contents

Several organizations have created booklets advising which items to put into survival packs. You'll find them online by searching "disaster preparedness" on your computer. Here are three I've found useful:

- *http://www.ready.gov/*

- *http://www.redcross.org/what-we-do/international-services/disaster-preparedness*

- *http://www.aspca.org/pet-care/disaster-preparedness*

The following pictures show what I have in my car.

You'll need to come up with what *you* should have.

References:

[1] *http://energy.gov/energysaver/articles/estimating-appliance-and-home-electronic-energy-use*

[2] Centers for Disease Control and Prevention *http://www.cdc.gov/co/*

Here's my three-day pack along with a list of its contents. Hanging from the straps are two Paracord Ropes and a water filtration bottle.

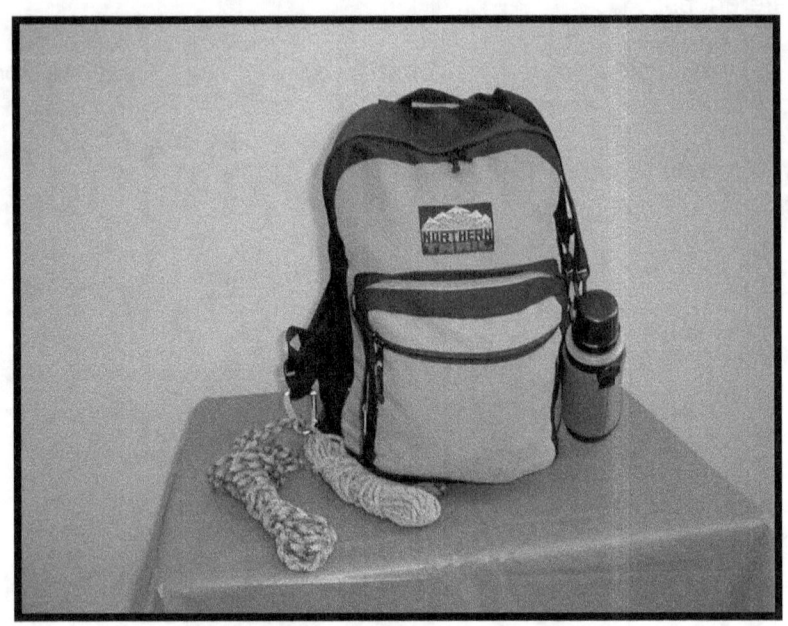

Basic Three-Day Pack

Very important: make sure all food is in hard plastic or metal containers. Rodents can invade your car and once the food is gone, they'll begin eating your car – voice of experience here! They love pet food and will even chew through water bottles to get what they need. What a mess!

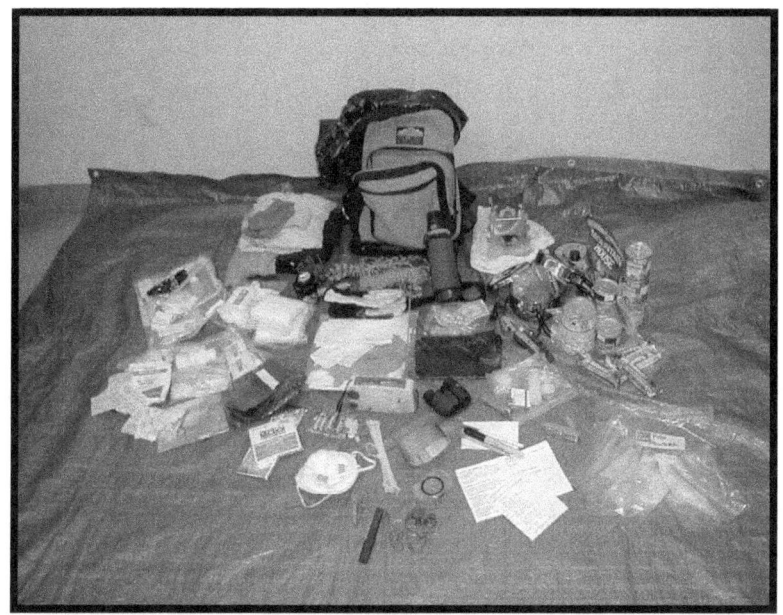

Basic Three - Day Pack Contents

Every kit is lined with a large plastic garbage bag to keep contents dry.

Basic Three-Day Pack Contents
(Expiration dates in parenthesis)

Attached to pack: purifier bottle, paracord rope [1]
(See references below)

Outer Pockets
- List of contents of 3-Day Pack
- List of contents of all backpacks
- List of contacts & directions
- Pocketknife, compass, 2 space blankets [2]
- Zip ties, poncho, whistle, magnesium fire starting tool [3]

75

- Chapstick, sunglasses, goggles, ear plugs
- Pad, pencil, pen, permanent marker
- Dust mask, small flashlight, signaling mirror [4]

Inner Pack
- Emergency radio (solar, hand-crank), 6 AA batteries (2017)
- Flashlight, headlamp (batteries removed and stored separately), extra batteries
- Fireproof matches, candles, cotton, Bic lighter
- Duct tape, leather gloves, 2 large garbage bags
- Binoculars
- Cash and Coins

Personal Items
- Camp soap, toothbrush w/ cover, tooth paste, floss
- 2 handiwipe towels, "1-2-3" towels, 2 small toilet paper rolls
- Chapstick, tissues, comb, nail file, clippers, tweezers
- Contact lens cleaner (2015), lens case, small mirror
- Disposable gloves, 3 handkerchiefs
- Poo Powder®, plastic bags

Health / Vitamins / Nutrition   (expiration date)
- Calcium Magnesium 1000 mg (2016) (for muscle aches and spasms)
- B1 400 mg (2015) (for use to relieve stress)
- Echatin (2015) (cold and sinus infection prevention)
- B12 packets (2015) (energy booster)

Personal First Aid
- Pain reliever (2016), cloves (for toothache)
- Band-aids, gauze pads, alcohol swabs
- Scissors, disposable gloves

Food / Cooking (expiration date)
- Nesting Mess Kit [5]
- Small, folding, P38 military can opener
- Eating utensils
- EmberLit portable wood stove (see Resources chapter)
- 3 cans chicken breast (2015) in zip plastic bags [6]
- 3 cans meat product (2016)
- 3 cans spaghetti (all empty cans could be useful!)
- Dehydrated peas and corn (2016) (can be eaten dry)
- 4 protein bars (2015), packets: coffee, tea, sugar
- 8 bouillon cubes (2015) (great for quick, hot, hydrating soup)

Clothing
- 3 underwear, 3 pairs socks, t-shirt, long johns, sweat pants, pants, shirt

Seasonal
- Mosquito netting, head net, repellant
- Sunscreen, cooling neck ties
- Gloves, hat, scarf

Notes & References:

[1] Paracord: *http://en.wikipedia.org/wiki/Parachute_cord*

[2] Space blanket: also known as a Mylar or emergency blanket: *http://en.wikipedia.org/wiki/Space_blanket*

[3] Magnesium fire-starting tool: *http://www.rei.com/product/407152/magnesium-fire-starting-tool*

[4] How to use a signaling mirror: *http://adventure.howstuffworks.com/survival/gear/use-signal-mirror.htm*

[5] A "nesting mess kit" is used for campsite cooking and eating. It often includes 1 or 2 pots, a frying pan, lid, a plate and a cup. All pieces stack and store within the pot.

[6] Pop top cans are very convenient, but what if they leak? I pack each can in its own zip plastic bag – just in case.

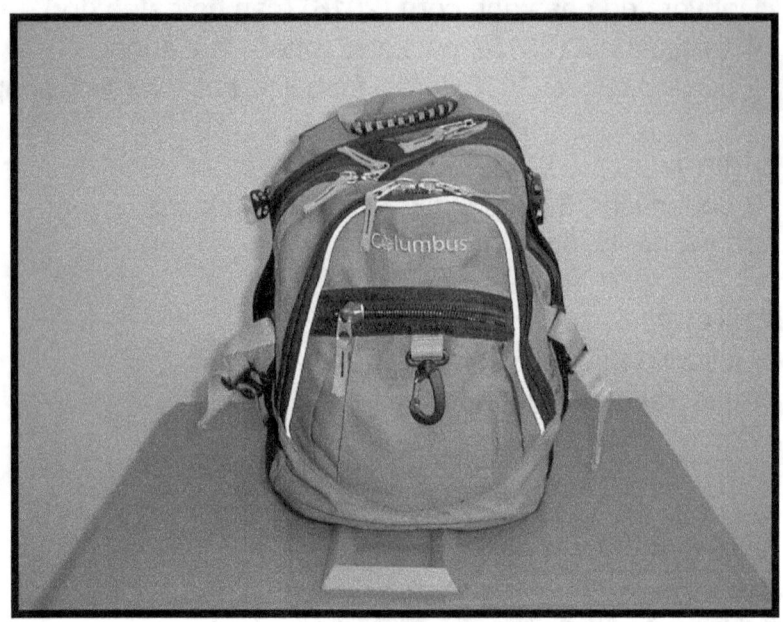

Extra Pack

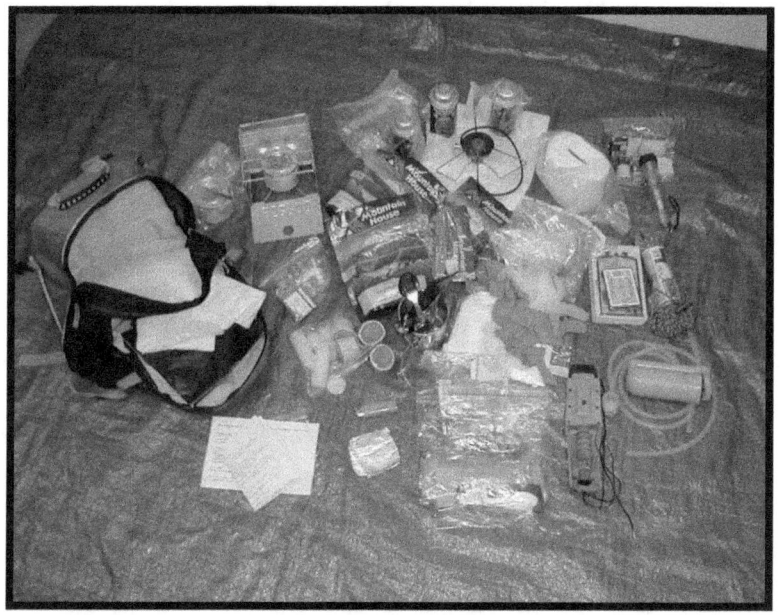

Extra Pack Contents

Extra Pack Contents
(Expiration dates in parenthesis)

Outer Pockets
- List of contents of Extra Pack
- List of contents of all backpacks
- List of contacts & directions

Middle Pocket
- Sterno stove, 2 fuel: screwdriver to open sterno cans
- Butane camp stove, 4 cans fuel
- Fire starter, matches, foil, candles, Bic lighter
- Metal cup, eating utensils
- Garbage bags, plastic bags, standard can opener

- Water purifier, camping knife, paracord [1]
- Battery-free shake flashlight [2]
- Toilet paper, tissues, disposable gloves
- Book, cards

Inner Pocket

- <u>Freeze Dried Dinners</u>   <u>Best by</u>
  Chicken Stew   7/15
  Chicken Teriyaki w/ Rice   6/16
  Spaghetti w/ Meat Sauce   7/15
  Scrambled Eggs w/ Bacon   8/15
- Packets: coffee, tea, sugar, salt
- Bouillon cubes (2016)

<u>References:</u>

[1] *http://en.wikipedia.org/wiki/Parachute_cord*

[2] *http://www.shake-flashlights.com/how-they-work.html*

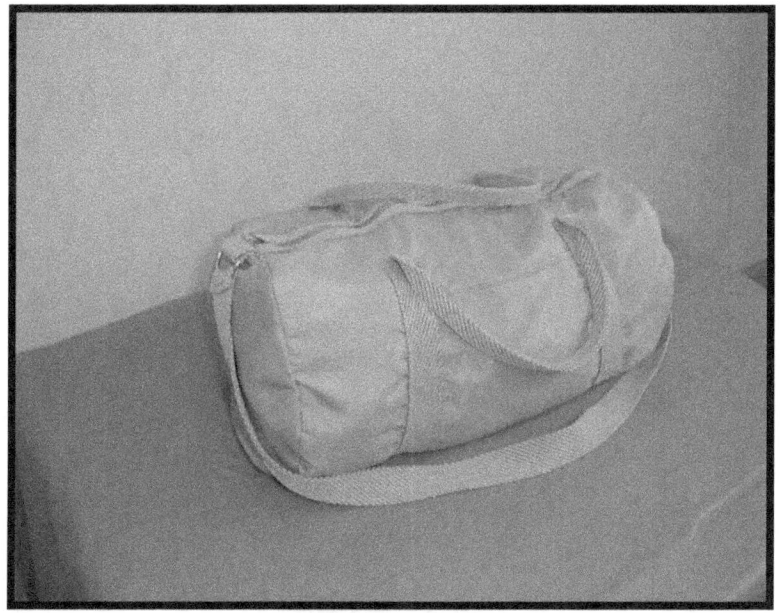

Pet Food Kit

Pet Food Kit Contents

Pet Food Kit Contents
(Expiration dates)

- List of contents of Pet Food Kit
- List of contents of all backpacks
- List of contacts & directions

Dry food re-sealable bag (2016)
- 8 Canned food (2015)
- 4 plastic dishes
- Paper plates
- Paper towels, spoon, knife
- Can opener

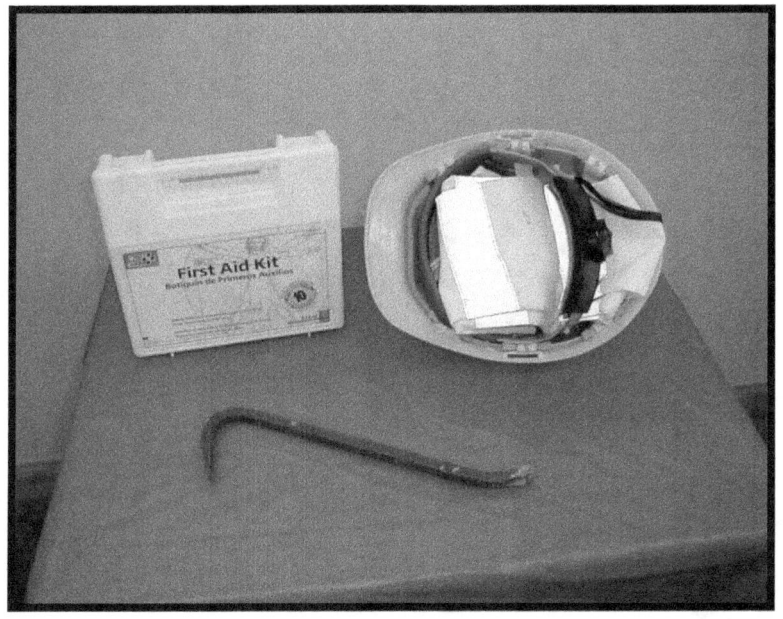

CERT "Kit"

A standard First Aid Kit, crowbar and CERT kit.

CERT Kit Contents

CERT Kit Contents

– Hard hat, safety vest
– Leather gloves, goggles
– Headlamp, batteries
– Crescent wrench (to turn off gas furnace)
– Duct tape, masking tape, box cutter
– Rite-in-the-rain (weather-resistant) journal & pen, pencil
– Permanent markers: red, black, green, yellow

Trunk Contents

In addition to the packs, you'll see a few other items. They're useful to me where I live. Pack what *you* can use.

- Camp shovel, hatchet, 2 tarps, bucket with lid
- Sleeping bag, sleeping pad,
- Fluorescent lantern, Luci Lite
- Air pump
- Winter coat, tennis shoes
- 3 gallons water (2016)
- Tool Box
    - o Electrical tape, duct tape, zip ties
    - o Nails, screws, tent stakes
    - o Hammer, screwdrivers, pliers, adjustable crescent wrench (to turn off gas)
    - o Box cutter, clamps, bungee cords

85

This is what it looks like all packed up:

Pack it up. Stow it in your car. Now.

CHAPTER 12

Guests in Your Car

I F YOU ARE JUST BEGINNING to prepare your car to be a valuable emergency asset, please keep in mind: it's very doable. Yes, there's a lot to think about (and better yet, DO), but doing a little bit each week will get you there.

If there's a shortcoming in this book, it's that in each situation you've been the only occupant in your car. Well, I did that deliberately. Now let's look to your guests.

Kids, friends, pets, grandparents – you know your regular passengers, and they'll all need help at the time of a disaster. You have the basics; now apply them to the people in your life.

How many people usually ride with you? Who is a usual passenger in your car?

What will happen if a disaster occurs when:

- You and a friend are going to dinner – in your car.

- You're driving neighborhood kids to or from baseball practice.

- You're taking your dogs to the park.

- You're driving your sick grandmother to her doctor appointment.

- You're taking your cat to the vet across town.

It's never been a problem before: you drive everyone there and take everyone home. Just routine, all is safe.

But one day it isn't safe. Driving to or from a place with a carload of people, some emergency occurs that prevents you from reaching your destination. And you have all these people or children or pets in your car.

How will your friend react to the emergency?

What will it be like, having the baseball team in your car for hours or days?

How will your pets act if not given food or water or kept in a carrier for days or longer?

Does your grandmother have all her daily medications with her?

Is it your fault that a disaster strikes? Certainly not. Could any sane person expect you to make disaster preparations for the people who ride in your car? Well now….

I look at my car the same way I view my home: it's my castle. That castle may have four wheels, but I'm still responsible for what happens in and around it, including anyone riding inside.

Whether you agree with that or not, picture it: you're stranded in the car with others – *your* friends, relatives or children. Can you see yourself unpacking a can of food from your kit – without offering any to them – really?

I'm sure you can imagine such scenarios and I heartily encourage you to do so. Think it through: what should you have in your car – for everyone?

I was thinking of this very thing one day when friends visited me with their three-month-old daughter. I'd known the couple for years, and now their family included a beautiful little girl. On this particular visit, the child was fretful and fussy. Noisy. Crying. Nothing helped until Mom gave her a bottle. Wow, what a relief it was – not just to hear silence again, but also to know the baby wasn't hurting or in need.

Now transfer that scene into your car. You're *in your car* with this family, something happens and you can't get home. The baby formula is soon gone – how are you going to explain to a three-month-old baby that there is no food?

Having adults with you is different. They'll understand you have limited resources to share with them when they have **none**. But children will just react – loudly.

The first decision to make in an emergency situation is: should you stay or leave? In the above examples, if you and everyone in your car stayed right there, what kind of night would it be? What kind of host would you be?

If you had to leave – and you would soon have to if you didn't have enough supplies for everyone, would everyone make it? What kind of leader would you be?

Some solutions to consider:

- In chapter six I mentioned having multiple kits in my car. Consider doing the same for kids and pets. My extra pack was created to hold items I might *not* need, but also to store extra food that others *might* need.

- Your family could make a project out of this. Each child could have his own small backpack with necessities for a disaster scenario. What will your children eat – right from the can or box? You see it's the same question you asked yourself when you put *your* pack together.

- If your pet is a regular passenger, pack a small duffle bag with food and dishes and make sure you have plenty of water to share!

- For the adults who are regular passengers, get them involved. Present them with this information and see if they will jump aboard the preparedness game.

When you go to the mall with your friend, Jill, it should be routine for her to bring a survival pack along. It might not have all the extras she has in *her* car, but it would be enough to get her through three days in yours.

Not only would she not be dependent on your supplies, she'd also have the survival mindset needed to successfully get through the emergency.

Which would you rather have as a passenger in a disaster: a partner or a victim?

What is in your car?

CHAPTER 13

Think it Through

L AST YEAR I WAS TALKING to a computer tech who was installing some software on my computer, and we discovered a mutual interest in preparedness issues. Waiting for the program to download, we discussed some of the actions we'd taken. He told me that his whole family, including wife and two young children had "bug-out bags" at their house. He had one too – at home.

There's a well-known bridge in my area, popularly called "the trestle" that crosses over a river and two sloughs. It's about two miles long and I knew he drove over it on his way to work – every day.

I asked him "If you were away from your house, on the other side of the trestle when an earthquake occurred and the trestle was damaged, how would you get home? And how long do you think it would it take you?"

We talked about alternate routes – all involving bridges that could also be damaged, and he concluded it could take several days to get home. When I explained the concept of turning your car into an emergency asset, he quickly realized where his survival pack should be: in the car, not at home.

Being prepared isn't all about widespread disasters. Haven't you already been "inconvenienced" by some sort of event – sitting in a car for a lot longer than you'd planned? Having to detour around construction, adding miles and minutes to your commute?

A protein bar, peanut butter crackers or a bag of nuts can help with sinking blood sugar levels and make a positive difference to emotions and your sense of well being.

And water – don't forget the value of water! It dilutes toxins, removes them from the body and aids circulation. If you don't drink enough water your brain can't function well, causing decreased concentration. You can suffer from headaches, migraines, tiredness or plain old crankiness!

Put some healthy snacks and water in your car. Right now!

I was driving on the freeway last winter when traffic slowed and stopped. Glancing over to the car next to me I saw a young woman wearing a sheer blouse. I could picture a short skirt and heels completing her attire. It didn't matter that it was forty degrees outside. She was in a warm car and when she got to work she'd probably park in an underground garage, take the elevator up to the fourth floor and step into a cozy, warm office building.

What if that scenario changed? What if she was stuck on the freeway while first responders attended to a huge wreck?

Television newscasts have shown cars abandoned in blizzard conditions on major highways across the United States. When the road became completely gridlocked, people couldn't move their cars so they moved their bodies – they walked out.

Picture that young woman walking anywhere!

If *you* are that woman, might there be a warm coat you never wear anymore lurking in your closet? Don't toss it to the thrift stores: consider putting it into a clean trash bag and storing it in your car – in the trunk, behind the seat, anywhere! And shoes: used tennis shoes, rain or snow boots – stick an old pair into a bag and put it in your car. You may really need walking shoes some day.

There are two issues we haven't covered yet and both of them have to do with health.

How healthy is your car? Can you depend on it in an emergency situation? How are the tires; has the oil been changed lately? And gas: do you keep the tank at least half full at all times?

The other health issue is you. Have you been putting off a trip to the dentist? (Want to have a raging toothache during an emergency evacuation?) How fit are you?

First aid kits are valuable and your car should own one, but remember: they are generic and won't have everything *you* need and want. What if you get stuck somewhere without your heart medication or a certain homeopathic remedy? What about a sinus infection, cold or migraine headache?

Let's say a landslide prevents you from getting home. Whether you're living in your car, at a shelter or at a friend's house, even a non life-threatening condition can make you awfully uncomfortable.

No matter how healthy you are, illness and pain can occur. Whatever medication you feel you need, put some into your disaster kit.

What do you have in your car?"

CHAPTER 14

With Knowledge Comes Responsibility

E'VE COVERED A LOT of ground to this point and I think you have the information to go forward on your own.

Preparing your car won't be a quick start-to-finish project; it will likely be an evolution. Start now instead of later, with something better than what you have in your car right now.

If you can take care of yourself, no one else has to take care of you.

The time will come when you feel comfortable letting friends or family know you've read this book and are preparing your car for a possible emergency. No matter how intelligent they are, you're going to be surprised when some reject the entire concept. If that happens, take it easy: you won't change minds by ramming these ideas down their throats. (And if every time they see you, you climb on a soapbox, things could get sticky indeed.)

Perhaps you could present this book to them as a gift. Let them read through it at their own pace and have their own realizations.

Don't neglect telling those who are already involved in prepping. I've met quite a few in varying levels of preparedness, and was shocked to learn that none had equipped their cars. When asked, most said *they just hadn't thought about it* – which is the reason for this guide.

I heartily encourage you to reach out and let others know, because when a disaster situation happens, many will either be uncomfortable or in serious peril.

Not so long ago, wearing seatbelts wasn't customary. When getting into someone's car you waited to see if the driver was going to belt up – it was his car and you followed his lead. If the driver said buckle up, that's what you did – even if you didn't want to.

In a model world everyone would have a small disaster kit that would travel with them when in someone else's car. No one would feel silly or self conscious about it, they'd just do it.

When I travel in another's car I ask if can bring my survival pack with me. I stress that it's just a small backpack and have never been told no. That's a great place to start and it often leads to a conversation that can result in *that* person getting more prepared.

You could start a whole new trend.

You may have noticed I say *"when"* a disaster happens, not *"if"* a disaster happens. That's because in looking around the planet I've seen thousands of people impacted by a disaster at one time or another. And some are hit with one right *after* the other!

Being prepared just makes sense.

You are responsible for you.

Wherever you are, you are.

And more often than not, wherever you are, you're near your car.

A Request

The purpose of this guide was to provide you with information, inspiration and encouragement as you better prepare for disasters.

If you have questions or suggestions for future editions, feel free to contact me at http://DJCastleBooks.com.

Also, please consider returning to the site where you purchased this guide and leave your feedback on this current work. Your input will be greatly appreciated!

Best,
DJ Castle

Acknowledgements

This guide would not have been written or published without the encouragement, writing ability and editing skill of Brian A. Brooks. Mentor, colleague, first (and only) ex-husband and all around best friend, his tireless efforts helped me turn ideas into a readable book format. And we had fun doing it.

I also want to thank and acknowledge two talented, professionals who helped with putting the important final touches on this guide.

Maria (Foster) Hicks has been a friend and business associate for many years. Formatting, printing and design issues that most people struggle with are intuitive for her and she played an integral part in preparing this book for printing. Maria is a third-generation printer and Operations Manager at her family's print shop in the Pacific Northwest. She can be reached at maria.hicks@fosterpress.com.

Natasha Fletcher's help was invaluable in designing the book cover. Her skill was surpassed only by her patience! Natasha is an aspiring designer and freelance writer who resides in the Pacific Northwest. She can be contacted at: FletcherCNatasha@yahoo.com

About The Author

DJ Castle is a preparedness advocate and has been involved with prepping throughout her entire adult life. She has owned an emergency kit company, written dozens of articles and belongs to several prepper clubs.

Her disaster planning education and training has included seminars conducted by the Red Cross and Emergency Management Service organizations in Washington State and in 2012 she completed a Community Emergency Response Team (CERT) program.